Primer diccionario ilustrado
Animales

First Picture Dictionary
Animals

Cerdo
Pig

Mariposa
Butterfly

Conejo
Rabbit

Zorro
Fox

Ilustrado por Anna Ivanir

www.kidkiddos.com
Copyright ©2025 by KidKiddos Books Ltd.
support@kidkiddos.com

All rights reserved. No part of this book may be reproduced in any form or by any electronic or mechanical means, including information storage and retrieval systems, without written permission from the publisher, except in the case of a reviewer, who may quote brief passages embodied in critical articles or in a review.
First edition, 2025

Library and Archives Canada Cataloguing in Publication
First Picture Dictionary – Animals (Spanish English Bilingual edition)
ISBN: 978-1-83416-261-4 paperback
ISBN: 978-1-83416-262-1 hardcover
ISBN: 978-1-83416-260-7 eBook

Animales salvajes
Wild Animals

León
Lion

Tigre
Tiger

Jirafa
Giraffe

✦ *Una jirafa es el animal terrestre más alto.*
✦ A giraffe is the tallest animal on land.

Elefante
Elephant

Mono
Monkey

Animales salvajes
Wild Animals

Hipopótamo
Hippopotamus

Panda
Panda

Zorro
Fox

Rinoceronte
Rhino

Ciervo
Deer

Alce
Moose

Lobo
Wolf

✦ *¡Un alce es un gran nadador y puede bucear para comer plantas!*

✦ *A moose is a great swimmer and can dive underwater to eat plants!*

Ardilla
Squirrel

Koala
Koala

✦ *¡Una ardilla esconde nueces para el invierno, pero a veces olvida dónde las puso!*

✦ *A squirrel hides nuts for winter, but sometimes forgets where it put them!*

Gorila
Gorilla

Mascotas
Pets

Canario
Canary

✦ *¡Una rana puede respirar por la piel y por los pulmones!*
✦ *A frog can breathe through its skin as well as its lungs!*

Cuy
Guinea Pig

Rana
Frog

Hámster
Hamster

Pez dorado
Goldfish

Perro
Dog

◆ *¡Algunos loros pueden copiar palabras e incluso reírse como los humanos!*

◆ *Some parrots can copy words and even laugh like a human!*

Gato
Cat

Loro
Parrot

Animales de la granja
Animals at the Farm

Vaca
Cow

Gallina
Chicken

Pato
Duck

Oveja
Sheep

Caballo
Horse

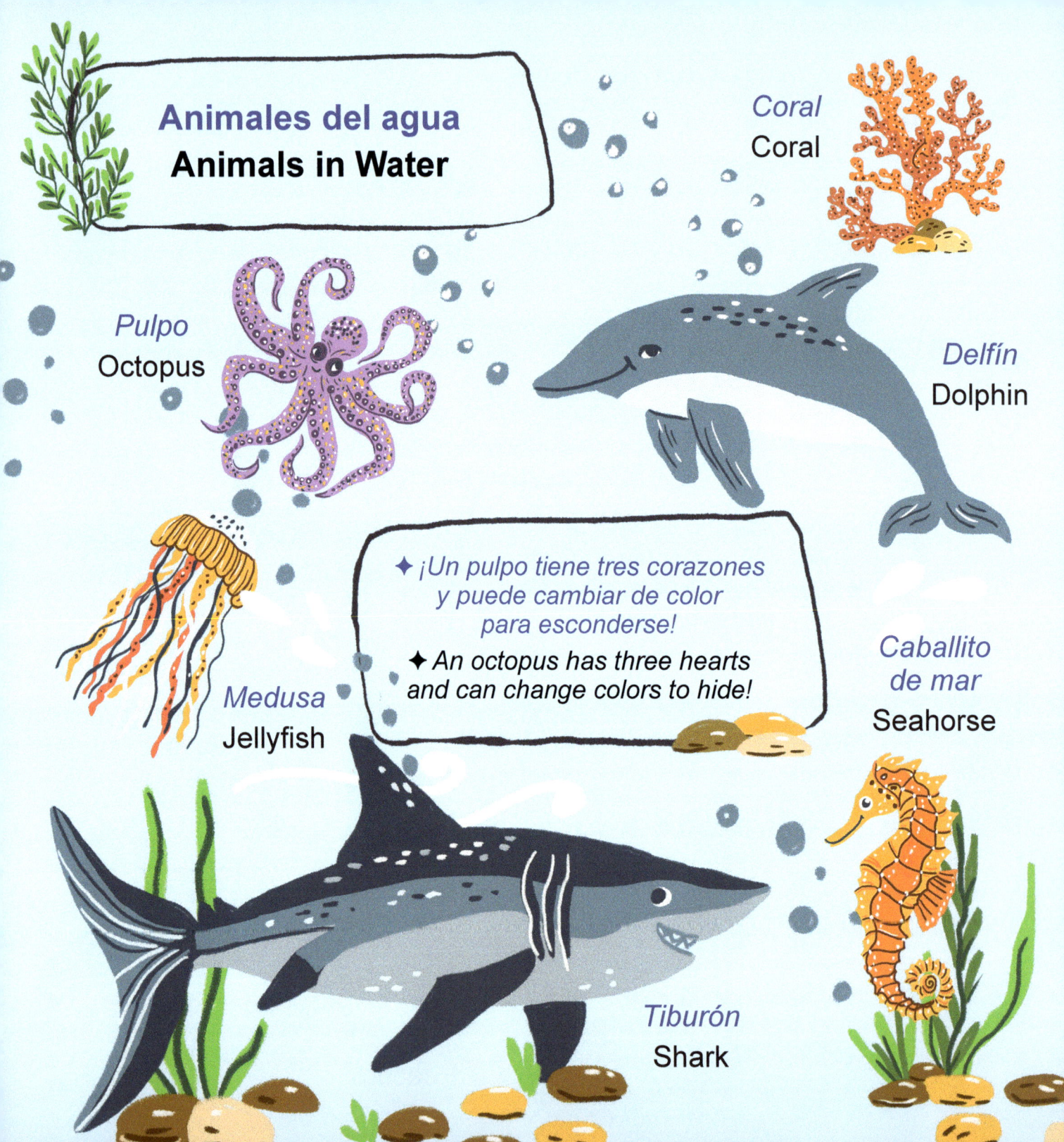

Tejón
Badger

Puercoespín
Porcupine

Marmota
Groundhog

✦ *¡Una lagartija puede volver a crecer su cola si la pierde!*
✦ A lizard can grow a new tail if it loses one!

Lagartija
Lizard

Hormiga
Ant

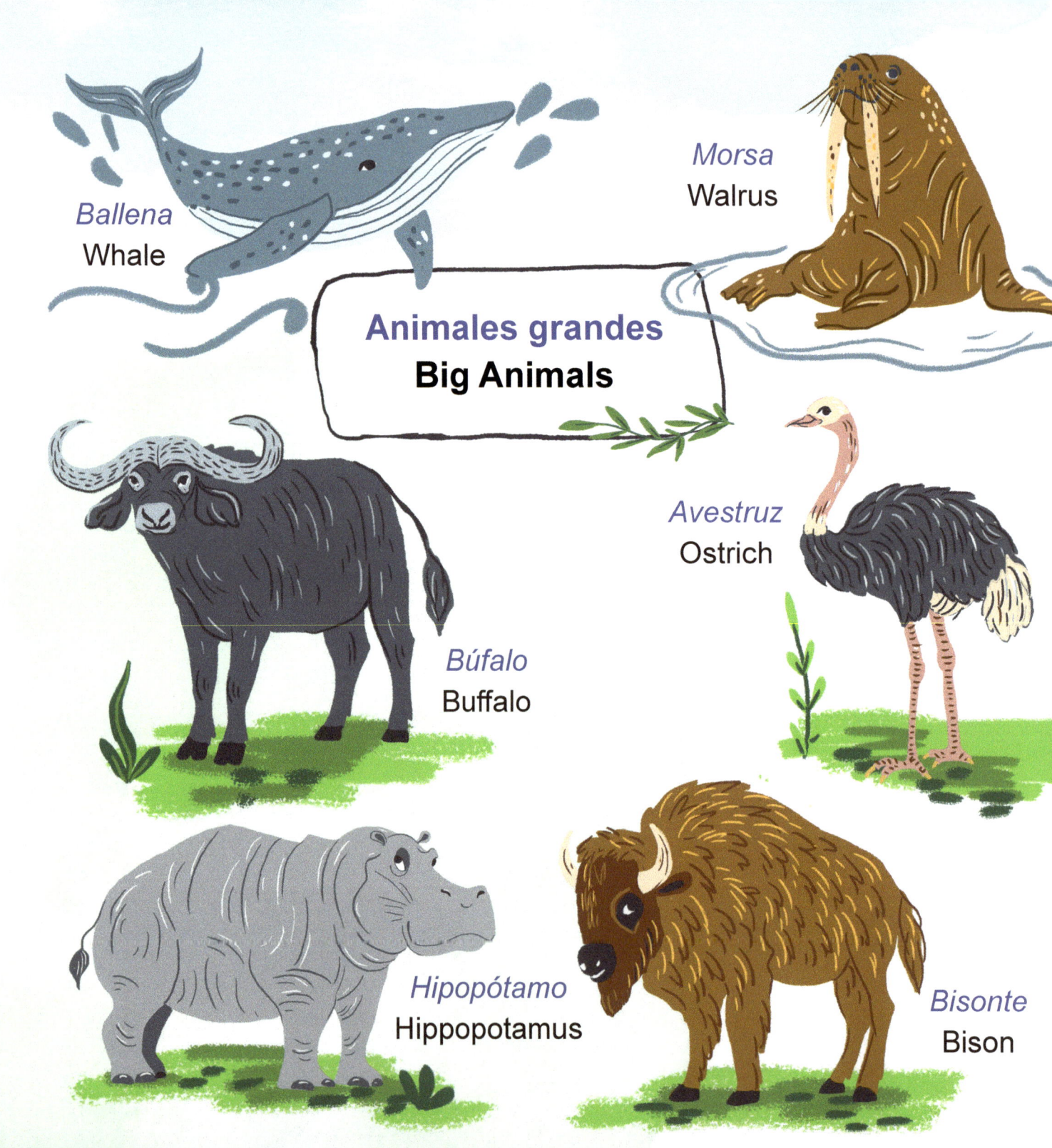

Animales pequeños
Small Animals

Camaleón
Chameleon

Araña
Spider

✦ *¡Un avestruz es el ave más grande, pero no puede volar!*
✦ *An ostrich is the biggest bird, but it cannot fly!*

Abeja
Bee

✦ *Un caracol lleva su casa en la espalda y se mueve muy lentamente.*
✦ *A snail carries its home on its back and moves very slowly.*

Caracol
Snail

Ratón
Mouse

Animales silenciosos
Quiet Animals

Tortuga
Turtle

Mariquita
Ladybug

✦ *Una tortuga puede vivir en la tierra y en el agua.*
✦ A turtle can live both on land and in water.

Pez
Fish

Lagartija
Lizard

Búho
Owl

Murciélago
Bat

✦ *Un búho caza de noche y usa el oído para encontrar su comida!*
✦ An owl hunts at night and uses its hearing to find food!

✦ *Una luciérnaga brilla en la noche para encontrar otras luciérnagas.*
✦ A firefly glows at night to find other fireflies.

Mapache
Raccoon

Tarántula
Tarantula

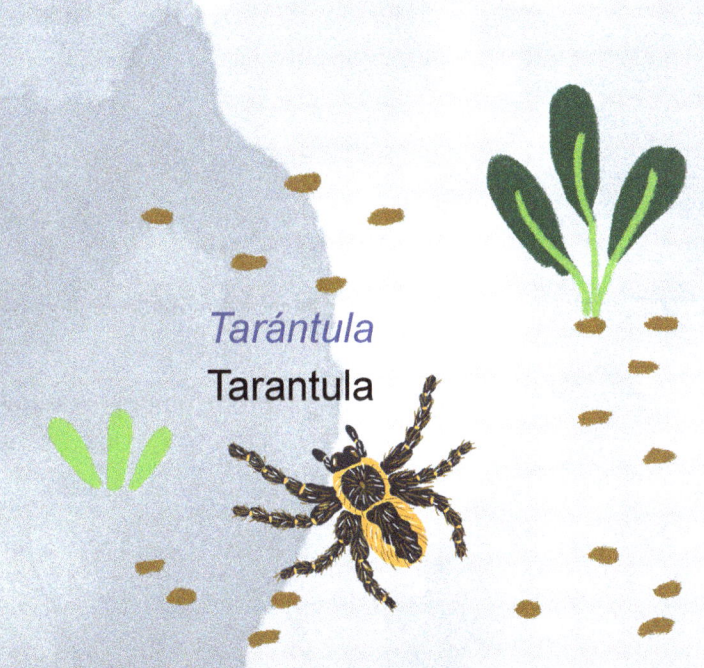

Animales coloridos
Colorful Animals

El flamenco es rosa
A flamingo is pink

El búho es marrón
An owl is brown

El cisne es blanco
A swan is white

El pulpo es morado
An octopus is purple

La rana es verde
A frog is green

> ✦ *Una rana es verde, entonces puede esconderse entre las hojas.*
> ✦ A frog is green, so it can hide among the leaves.

El oso polar es blanco
A polar bear is white

El zorro es naranja
A fox is orange

El koala es gris
A koala is grey

La pantera es negra
A panther is black

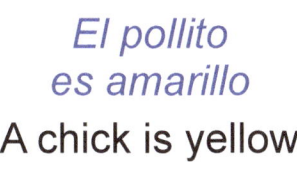

El pollito es amarillo
A chick is yellow

Animales y sus crías
Animals and Their Babies

Vaca y Ternero
Cow and Calf

Gato y Gatito
Cat and Kitten

Gallina y Pollito
Chicken and Chick

✦ *Un pollito habla con su mamá antes de nacer.*
✦ *A chick talks to its mother even before it hatches.*

Perro y Cachorro
Dog and Puppy

Mariposa y Oruga
Butterfly and Caterpillar

Oveja y Cordero
Sheep and Lamb

Caballo y Potro
Horse and Foal

Cerdo y Cerdito
Pig and Piglet

Cabra y Cabrito
Goat and Kid

www.ingramcontent.com/pod-product-compliance
Lightning Source LLC
LaVergne TN
LVHW072103060526
838200LV00061B/4797